THE SACRED
GARDEN

THE SACRED GARDEN
SOIL FOR THE GROWING SOUL

Patricia R. Barrett

MOREHOUSE PUBLISHING

Copyright © 2000 by Patricia R. Barrett

Morehouse Publishing
P.O. Box 1321
Harrisburg, PA 17105

Morehouse Publishing is a division of The Morehouse Group.

The Scripture quotations contained herein are from the New Revised Standard Version Bible copyright © 1989 by the Division of Christian Education of the National Council of the Churches of Christ in the U.S.A. Used by permission. All rights reserved.

Printed in the United States of America

Cover design by Dana Jackson
Cover image: English Country Garden, Suffolk
              CORBIS/Clay Perry

Library of Congress Cataloging-in-Publication Data

Barrett, Patti, 1949-
    The sacred garden : soil for the growing soul / Patricia R. Barrett.
        p. cm.
    ISBN 0-8192-1831-6 (pbk. : alk. paper)
    1. Gardens—Religious aspects—Christianity—Meditations. 2. Gardening—Religious aspects—Christianity—Meditations. 3. Spiritual life—Episcopal Church. I. Title.

    BT695.5 .B373 2000
    242—dc21

                                                                    99-057683

To my friends
the Sisters of the Order of St. Anne at Bethany
whose gardens invite you to prayer

CONTENTS

With the song of the birds for pardon
And the joy of the flowers for mirth
One is nearer God's heart in a garden
Than anywhere else on earth.

I was lucky enough to inherit this verse, embroidered and framed, from my husband's grandmother. I think I have read it nearly each day for the past thirty years and am always struck by its simple truth. The garden where we find God's heart does not have to be complicated or of intricate design but can be simply a place outdoors where we like to be, where we are nearer to God.

From the time I was a young girl, being in a garden nourished me and deepened my awareness of the natural world and my place in it. The smells and colors of my grandmother's circular perennial beds, filled with tall, showy phlox of every color, still haunt me. Images of my grandmother, the flowers, and the love and caring that I felt come back to me as I tend my own phlox. The past and the present are connected in a deeply spiritual way.

I started writing about gardens as a young mother, when I spent a great deal of time in my country home. Raising my two daughters in an old farmhouse led to planting vegetables and flowers and marveling at the way everything grew and flourished even when we felt we didn't know what we were doing. We learned the names of all the plants and helped them to grow, and then we ventured out into the fields around our home and began to know the wild-flowers, exploring all of nature's beauty.

As my children grew, and I became busier with less time to spend in the garden, the images I had found there kept coming back to me in my prayers. And when I went to the garden to do some chore or other, I realized I was in prayer. The solitude, the beauty, the smells, the feel of the total experience brought me closer to God and closer to my inner being. I settled in the garden. I could stop the fretting and simply be. God was close by, listening to me. And I, too, began to listen.

My writing about gardens led to other writing and other jobs. But my life didn't seem to be quite right. I still heard God; I still listened. Eventually, I acted on it. I attended seminary and will soon be ordained as an Episcopal deacon and then, priest. I began writing this book of meditations in seminary. It came out of my own prayer life, which had its own seasons, sometimes similar to that of a rather unkempt garden.

I wrote this book for all who find garden images alive in their heart. Connection with gardens, even small ones, even potted plants, can become windows to the inner life. The simple act of stopping and looking at the beauty around us can be prayer. The quiet of a garden gives of itself and the taking from it becomes an instant blessing.

This book is divided by seasons, but the thoughts and meditations on the Bible verses can work anytime during the year. As you read, you can imagine a garden or visualize a garden you know. I hope the words and the prayers and the stillness you will find will draw you into the garden of your heart. Find rest and nourishment in this garden. Let it speak to you. Explore the space and share it with the Creator. Let God into your garden, into your heart.

Spring

Those who love me, I will deliver; I will protect those who know my name.
Psalm 91:14

S pring often begins with cool, moist weather. It may still be frosty in parts of the country, so planting has to be slow, but the soil will soon be dry enough to work. I like to begin the garden season by removing the winter covers of mulch from the perennials, biennials, and spring-flowering bulbs.

Removing the thick blanket of now-soggy leaves from around the plants, I can see new growth peeking out. Carefully, so as not to hurt the new shoots, I peel back the covering. Even though there is still a slight chill in the air, the warmth of the early spring sun fills me with a comfort and a promise that I had almost forgotten.

Dear Creator God, help me uncover the secret desires and yearnings of my own heart this spring. Keep me warm without the coverings I use to protect myself from the daily stings and abuses that come my way. Instead, let me revel in the spring promise and know that you alone provide all the sustenance I need to see me through the months ahead.

And can any of you by worrying add a single hour to your span of life?
Matthew 6:27

T ime to go to the vegetable garden and make sure the soil is ready for planting. The frost is off the earth and the soil can be raked; the rocks that seem to spring from somewhere deep within the earth need to be collected and removed so that there will be pure, rich garden loam once again. Raking and smoothing the soil is necessary before planting or transplanting anything into the garden so the roots can grow freely without becoming entangled in any impediments.

❧

Raking is meditative work. Captured in the moment when nothing is as important as what I am doing now, the act of pushing this soil and gathering these rocks occupies all my thoughts. Other thoughts and worries are buried as I wonder about these rocks and why they keep appearing in spite of the number I remove each spring.

Dear Mother/Father God, I am a lot like the rocks. My problems and worries keep appearing no matter how hard I work at removing them from the soil of my soul. Help me clear out my own mind and heart. Let me be like this earth, ready for new growth and new possibilities.

"I am the true vine, and my Father is the vinegrower. He removes every branch in me that bears no fruit. Every branch that bears fruit he prunes to make it bear more fruit."

John 15:1–2

The early mornings are still cold and it's a good time to prune the plants in the yard. The smaller gray-leafed and other dwarf evergreen shrubs, such as the lavenders, can be pruned too. Trim them back to encourage fresh, bushy growth from the base of the plants. This also keeps them from becoming too leggy and bare-looking later in the season.

Pruning—clipping away to get the shape I want—always feels a bit like reverse sculpting. Each cut removes dead wood and allows more room for the plant to breathe and grow. But how do we know what to trim, to eliminate and change? I am reminded of all the extras in my own life that I need to lessen so that I can become more wholly centered.

Help me, Beloved One, to know what I need to keep in my life and what I need to be strong enough to let go. With your guidance, perhaps I can be clearer and know what it is I need the most.

"And why do you worry about clothing? Consider the lilies of the field, how they grow; they neither toil nor spin.... But if God so clothes the grass of the field, which is alive today and tomorrow is thrown into the oven, will he not much more clothe you?"

Matthew 6:28–30

Early spring is a good time to plant raspberries in trenches. Pick a sunny, sheltered spot. Dig a trench about six inches wide and four inches deep. Set in the canes eighteen inches apart and cover the spread-out roots with soil, firming it in with your foot. Once you've planted the canes, cut them back to nine inches above the ground. Water well.

❧

I plant these young shoots and wonder how they will grow into bushy plants filled with red berries. They look so simple and insignificant right now. Will the soil and the nutrients and the sun and the rain transform them into healthy plants? How much help will they need from me? I am cared for, too, like these young plants.

*When I am thirsty or hungry I am cared
for by you, my Provider. You feed me with
prayer; I can feel you yearning for me as
I yearn for you. This endless craving for
the Other, this endless desire to be filled
is here within. I thank you for that blessing and pray that, like these simple canes,
I will flourish.*

"You are my friends if you do what I command you."
John 15:14

C lean out all flowerpots and get them ready for planting when the danger of frost is past. Take smaller pots inside and wash with warm water and a mild bleach solution; be sure to clean the outside as well as the interior. Larger pots can be hosed down outside but may need a wipe with bleach solution as well. Dry pots in the sun.

✷

Washing these old pots is a bit like being with old friends. Some of my big clay pots were my grandmother's, and I like to think of her filling them with her favorite blue and white flowers each summer. Now I clean them and repair their many cracks as best I can in the hopes they will last another year. These pots get heavy and are difficult to move around each spring, and yet I wouldn't think of getting rid of them. Each pot connects me to the past, connects me to all those saints who have gone before me.

Precious God, thank you for the communion of saints, who surround me and guide me with their gentle spirits. Recalling this never-ending fellowship of believers gives me solace and strength each day. Let me keep them close by and in my heart always.

Who will separate us from the love of Christ? Will hardship, or distress, or persecution, or famine, or nakedness, or peril, or sword?

Romans 8:35

It's time to divide some of the perennials that bloom later in the season. Divide those daylilies that didn't bloom well last year. Dig up the whole plant, be brave, and stick two pitchforks, back-to-back, into the clump of daylilies. Pull the forks apart until the plant separates. Plant the individual plants in loose, fertile soil that has been enriched with bone-meal, rock phosphate, or another high-phosphorous fertilizer.

❧

It feels good to work hard and to force my muscles to move against the roots of these old plants. I may be fighting nature in a way, but only so the plants will rejuvenate and have more room to really blossom.

Help me, God, untangle all the parts of myself that have become too entwined and confused. Let me realize what parts I need to nourish and what parts I may need to work on so that growth can occur. I open myself to you in prayer, Lord, and hold up what bothers me most and what I cannot quite figure out. I ask only that I may begin to know what it is that is so constricting, so inhibiting to my new growth. Help me here; help me flourish.

"A sower went out to sow. And as he sowed, some seed fell on the path, and the birds came and ate it up. Other seed fell on rocky ground, where it did not have much soil, and it sprang up quickly, since it had no depth of soil. And when the sun rose, it was scorched; and since it had no root, it withered away. Other seed fell among thorns, and the thorns grew up and choked it, and it yielded no grain. Other seed fell into good soil and brought forth grain, growing up and increasing and yielding thirty and sixty and a hundredfold."

Mark 4:3–8

Straight rows help make for good garden growth, as they allow proper spacing for the plants. You can plan in advance where you want what to grow. Mark out the rows with string before planting. Put markers at the ends of the row and stretch the string between the markers. Use a planting board to make the furrow for seeds that are small.

⚜

Pulling string in a garden can seem rather foolish. I am always tempted to simply throw the seeds in and let them grow as they may, and

I am sure some gardeners have success with this method. I am more careful than that—with my life as with the garden. If I plan, I can incorporate prayer more fully into my daily schedule. Spending time in prayer gives me assurance that my day will have some direction. Even if the day gets away from me, as it often does, I can think back to my prayer time, to my time with God, and derive comfort from that. I need to plan and help make things happen, as well as keep myself open to God's will.

Holy Spirit, help me with this. Come into my life. Help me see what is most important, and guide all my plans.

What are human beings that you are mindful of them, mortals that you care for them? Yet you have made them a little lower than God, and crowned them with glory and honor. You have given them dominion over the works of your hands; you have put all things under their feet.

Psalm 8:4–6

Crocus are out in abundance, adding color to what was such a bleak landscape. I planted quite a few last year, but the space still needs more. Note now on the fall months of your calendar where more bulbs should be planted. When the flowers of the crocus fade, cut them off at the base of the stem and fertilize with a 5-10-5 fertilizer to nourish the bulbs through their ripening period.

In the incredible busyness of day-to-day life, it is so simple to gaze at a flower and be stirred by its beauty. It is simple and yet it offers so much. More than six hundred years ago, St. Francis prayed, "My God and All, what are thou? And what am I?" We are still asking those questions today.

Lord, what am I when compared to this flower? What are you in giving this flower to me? How can I live my life to notice these simple gifts? The simple beauty of the flower stirs my need to know you better. I pray today, God, not to pretend to know you but to wait patiently as you reveal yourself to me over time.

O God, from my youth you have taught me, and I still proclaim your won-drous deeds. So even to old age and gray hairs, O God, do not forsake me.
                                                                    Psalm 71:17–18

S ow carrots in the early spring. Dig the soil over carefully at least eight inches deep, and remove any rocks that could hurt the carrots' growth. Put some good compost or a 5-10-5 fertilizer in the top six inches of soil. Then rake carefully. Mark the row and make about a half-inch fur-row in which to plant the seeds; space them a half-inch apart. This is dif-ficult as the seeds are very small. Carrots take about three weeks to germinate, so plant some radish seeds in with them to mark the row.

❦

Planting tiny seeds makes me want to scream; my patience is dimin-ished when it comes to dealing with things this small. Working with them, I can't help but notice my failing eyesight and lack of dexterity. I am all thumbs, and the seeds keep sticking to my fingers and don't go where I direct them. It is frustrating. I cannot control it, nor can I control my aging body, my failing eyes. No matter how many skin creams I buy, my skin still dries out. I have wrinkles now; my gums are receding. My body cramps after a day bent over like this.

Help me, Comforting God, accept who I am and the aging that goes along with my body. Let me stretch and remain as flexible in body as I try to be in spirit. Course through me and give me strength. This I ask in Jesus' name.

I pray that, according to the riches of his glory, he may grant that you may be strengthened in your inner being with power through his Spirit, and that Christ may dwell in your hearts through faith, as you are being rooted and grounded in love.

Ephesians 3:16–17

Roses are work, but they are worth it. Keep an eye on the roses now as they break into leaf and new shoots appear. Rising temperatures can also encourage aphids, so be careful to ward off pest attacks. Roses need quite a bit of food and water. Keep weeds away, as they just rob the plant of food. Mulch can keep moisture in the soil and reduce weeds. Apply about a two-inch layer of compost over the rose bed and leave a small ring of bare soil around the base of each plant.

❧

Roses. Their beauty astounds. But I can never look at the beauty of a rose without instantly realizing the spiritual nature of that which brought it about—God (or as some like to say, the creative principle). To meditate on this idea is to fill the soul with an abundance of awe.

Creator God, I go inward, with your help, to try to achieve the inner consciousness that is the higher consciousness I so long for. If I can achieve this, then perhaps I can begin to be aware of what lies just beyond my immediate knowledge. Patience. Trust. I ask for that, dear One; and for your help and guidance in achieving what only you know I desire.

The LORD will guide you continually, and satisfy your needs in parched places, and make your bones strong; and you shall be like a watered garden, like a spring of water, whose waters never fail.

Isaiah 58:11

S pring is the best time to plant evergreens so that they can establish themselves before summer begins. Give each plant plenty of room to grow and water thoroughly throughout the growing season. Because evergreens come in so many shapes and sizes, they can play an important role in establishing the "bones" of the garden, giving color and texture all year round.

❧

Planning the bones of a garden is difficult. It is easier to plant the masses of flowers for color and show than it is to figure out what should anchor the landscape all year long. That is true in my life as well. It is easier to plan the day-to-day activities, the "what am I doing today" list, than it is to plan the meatier, more important landscape of what I want my life to be.

I cannot make these plans alone, O God. I cannot achieve what I really want in life without you, without your help and your presence and your light. Help me begin to know what it is I want and long for, what my heart desires.

The human mind may devise many plans, but it is the purpose of the LORD that will be established.

Proverbs 19:21

Plant bunching onions in vegetable gardens now. Buy some sets at the local nursery and plant them, just covering the bulb. Onions like deep soil that is a bit sandy. Planting onions all around the perimeter of the garden will help repel woodchucks and rabbits.

❧

A border of onions standing guard around the garden gives it an orderly look. For a few months it actually looks as if I had planned it—with everything in its place and the neat, weed-free rows perfectly groomed. By midsummer, this neat plot will be overflowing with leaves and flowers and color and scent; nothing will be quite as planned. And yet the harvest is rich. Life is like that, too. The harvest is not always the one I expected. Sometimes my neatly organized plots get hit by a pest or natural disaster of some sort. As I seek to recover, however, I discover that God's love and guidance have been with me in the midst of what felt like chaos.

---✹---

*Gracious God, help me to understand
that my own plans may not always be
your plans, but that the harvest will be
rich anyway.*

You have given me the shield of your salvation, and your right hand has supported me; your help has made me great.

Psalm 18:35

S ow dill directly in the garden. Dill, with its tall lacy leaves and large seed heads, adds such a bright touch to the vegetable garden. It self-sows, too, but I like to plant a row of it to be used in flower arrangements as well as in cooking. Dill likes any well-drained garden soil as long as it gets sun. To sow, rake the earth and scatter a few seeds over it, cover about a quarter-inch deep, and keep moist. Plants grow three- to four-feet high. A few weeks later, sow more of this herb so fresh dill will be available all summer long. Plant dill near tomatoes to trap green tomato worms.

The idea of companion planting seems like a mystery, and yet it makes sense that one plant would help another somehow, that tomatoes would benefit from growing near dill or basil, for example. I, too, like to be near those people who make me better, who make me shine and see in me all I can be, even though I sometimes have trouble getting there.

Help me to be like those companion plants, God, and bring out the best in those who grow all around me.

Who are they that fear the LORD? He will teach them the way that they should choose.

Psalm 25:12

At the height of the planting season there is so much to do in the garden that it is difficult to know where to begin. If you have a vegetable garden, you may want to be sure it is well under way. Sow lettuce seeds in the garden early in the season or plant seedlings of lettuce already started at a garden center. Plant different varieties of leaf lettuce to make a colorful row as well as a beautiful salad.

❧

Sometimes at this time of year I am overwhelmed by all the planting, the rush of growth, and the myriad garden chores. It is then that I have to choose carefully what I want to do each day; otherwise I will be burdened by trying to do too much at once or by feeling I have to spend all day in the garden when I have other things to do. This is true not only with my garden, but with my life as a whole.

Dear Sustainer, help me to choose what will be most beneficial to do today in my garden and in my life. Give me wisdom to learn how to choose from all the possibilities before me, and give me the grace to carry out my plans to the best of my abilities.

Show for yourselves righteousness; reap steadfast love; break up your fallow ground; for it is time to seek the LORD, that he may come and rain righteousness upon you.

Hosea 10:12

After danger of frost has passed, sow basil seeds directly in the garden. Plant them in a half-inch furrow that you have enriched with manure and lime. Thin the seedlings in a few weeks and use the thinnings in salads. Basil makes a wonderful pesto, and it grows well in containers, too. Just give it lots of sun and keep it well fed.

❧

Oh, that life could be so easy! If only we came with such directions as "Just give her lots of sun and keep her well fed." Wouldn't that make things simpler? What would be the directions for growing me, I wonder? "Just give her lots of hugs and keep her well loved" or "Just give her lots of space and keep her well loved" or "Just give her lots of knowledge and keep her well loved." The "well loved" part is so important for my life. And in order to be well loved I need to love, to love freely and openly and without fear.

Help me with this today, my loving God. Help me be faithful to you and to know that there is nothing I can do to keep you from loving me.

For as the earth brings forth its shoots, and as a garden causes what is sown in it to spring up, so the Lord GOD will cause righteousness and praise to spring up before all the nations.

Isaiah 61:11

S ow carrots in the garden in the spring. Once they sprout, there is the tedious job of thinning the young plants to about one-inch intervals. You may be tempted not to do this, but it is important to give the plants room to grow. Carrots like a lot of water while they are growing and don't mind fertilizer. A handful of 5-10-5 to a five-foot row, scattered along both sides, usually works well.

❧

I don't enjoy jobs such as thinning the carrots. This kind of detail work is so time-consuming and painstaking, and it leaves my body tense and tired from bending over and carefully pulling out just the right number of young plants for the rest to grow well. So much of my time is filled with these tasks, not only in the garden but in all of my life. So much of the day is filled with tedium, the chores of day-to-day living, that it is easy to forget to find any joy in them. Still, details need to be taken care of, whether it's sorting the laundry or pulling these young seedlings. These jobs are important and worthwhile.

———————— ❧ ————————

Teach me to relax and enjoy this kind of work, Holy One. Help me to slow down and pay attention even when the work seems boring.

And the Lord *your God will make you abundantly prosperous in all your undertakings, in the fruit of your body, in the fruit of your livestock, and in the fruit of your soil. For the* Lord *will again take delight in prospering you.*

Deuteronomy 30:9

My pots, window boxes, and odd-shaped containers are ready to be filled with potting soil. I buy prepackaged soil, but you can make your own. A basic recipe for a good potting soil is one part peat moss, one part garden soil, and one part sand. Add a slow-release fertilizer to the mix so the plants get a gradual dose of nutrients as they grow. Mix the soil in your wheelbarrow, and store it in a large plastic container.

What fun it is to mix soil, to pour in the sand and to stir it all together as if I am making some kind of huge dough. I pull off my garden gloves so my hands can feel the earth—somehow it doesn't seem right unless the soil gets into my pores, under my nails, and all over my hands. One of my gardening teachers taught me early on never to call good garden soil "dirt" as it is the rich base on which all else depends. This soil is needed by everything that will blossom later in the season.

———————— ❧ ————————

Dear God, who gives this soil so that we can create a pleasing landscape, help me find the basics I need in prayer each day to feed what should grow in me. Let me seek wisdom and understanding in Scripture and in reading and listening to you. Give me the basics so that I can grow.

For you tithe mint and rue and herbs of all kinds, and neglect justice and the love of God; it is these you ought to have practiced, without neglecting the others.

Luke 11:42

O ne of the best parts of an herb garden is the wonderful scent the plants give off. This is a good time to plant annual herbs including parsley, marjoram, and summer savory. I plant unusual thymes each year as well as new plantings of lavender, which never does very well in our harsh winters. Try something new this spring, perhaps pineapple sage or opal basil.

❧

The scents of the herbs go right to my head, creating a certain nostalgia that I don't get in any of the other gardens. The lavender takes me back to my grandmother's house, where every drawer and closet was filled with lavender soap. I can see her in her tweed suit and big straw hat going into her garden, the first I ever knew, and cutting huge armfuls of phlox for the house. I can smell her here and I am overcome by the memories, not only of my grandmother, but of other people who once loved me. It is as if I can smell them into being again.

Let them be with me today, God. Let them be my angels when I need them the most.

Summer

For the law of the Spirit of life in Christ Jesus has set you free from the law of sin and of death.

Romans 8:2

Plant a window box. If you don't have one, make one or buy an inexpensive one. You will be amazed at how much joy a window box will give you and those who walk by your home. Try to place it on a window that you can see from the inside so you can enjoy the scents that are blown inside. A basic window box in a sunny spot can be filled with geraniums or with any combination of annuals or herbs. Shady spots work well for plantings of impatiens or lobelia or a mix of gray-leafed plants. Add something that cascades. Just remember that these boxes need frequent waterings and feedings to stay in good shape.

The window box gives me more joy than seems possible. I love the way the plants spill over the edge of the narrow container and hang down, showing a free spirit that cannot be contained.

Would that I, God, show the same spirit in parts of my life that need opening and freeing. Let me begin to let parts of my self go when the need is there—to free up those parts that long to grow a bit over the edge of my sometimes too restrained exterior. I ask for your help, my Sustainer, as I cannot do this alone.

They confronted me in the day of my calamity; but the LORD was my support.
Psalm 18:18

S taking is important in a flower garden. It takes a certain amount of respect and a bit of restraint to do it well. It is wise to stake plants early in their lives so they will be well supported when in full bloom. I use a wire ring atop wire stakes that I set over the young plant, pushing the stakes deep into the earth and pulling them up a bit as the plant grows.

On some days I would like to be able to ask you, God, for something like a stake to hold me up. Sometimes the pain of the world is too much; when I see too much suffering, I cry out for something to lean on. I long, too, for that same support for all of those in the world who live in pain. Perhaps that is why you gave me community, God. The image of people encircling me with their joined hands can be my stake, my support on days when I cannot do it alone.

"Say therefore to the Israelites, 'I am the LORD, and I will free you from the burdens of the Egyptians and deliver you from slavery to them. I will redeem you with an outstretched arm and with mighty acts of judgment.'"

Exodus 6:6

Given time, most houseplants will outgrow their pots. Repot any houseplants that look as if they need a new home. Choose a pot with a diameter one inch larger than the previous one. Remove plant from the original pot by tapping on the bottom, loosening dirt around the sides of the pot. Loosen the soil around the roots of the plant and remove any pieces of crockery that are stuck in the bottom of the soil. Put a thin layer of new soil in the bottom of the new pot, hold the plant in place in the new pot, and add soil, filling the pot to within a half-inch below the rim. Tap down firmly on all sides. Water well and place in a shaded spot to allow the plant to adjust to its new quarters.

Repotting is such a release; I can imagine the freedom these roots must feel as they escape the confines of their old existence. How do I know when I need to be released from my accustomed life? How long does it take for me to take the plunge into something unknown? How tightly confined do I have to be before I beg to be released?

Let me trust in you, God, and know that you support me as I leave behind old, confining spaces and seek new ones. Give me strength to grow strong and healthy in my new soil.

Happy are those who find wisdom, and those who get understanding, for her income is better than silver, and her revenue better than gold.
Proverbs 3:13–14

Geraniums are all over the place now, in supermarkets, in garden centers, and at plant sales. They are so easy to care for in containers or in a garden bed that gets a lot of sun. Tuck geraniums where you need a spot of color. Plant a tub filled with pink geraniums in the corner by the garage or plant some around the mailbox near the road. Remember to water during dry spells, feed occasionally to encourage flowering, and clip off spent blossoms. You'll be rewarded with bloom all summer long.

What a trusted plant the geranium is—so trustworthy that even gardeners who scoff at something so common can be caught planting a few where nothing else will work quite as well. Geraniums, with their vivid colors that attract hummingbirds and butterflies, just keep blooming all season long. So lovely, and so easy to take for granted.

Are there people in my life, God, whom I take for granted? What about those people who are always there when I need them and who keep up friendship under any circumstance, the ones I can always count on to listen to my problems. Have I told them lately what they mean to me? Or have I just treated them as ordinary occurrences in my life? Help me to remember those in my life who keep me going and whom I may take for granted. Let me remember to tell them what they mean to me. And let them be in my prayers, God. Let me thank you for their many gifts.

And make straight paths for your feet, so that what is lame may not be put out of joint, but rather be healed.

Hebrews 12:13

Edge the garden beds often during the garden year. A good-quality edging tool, nice and sharp, is perfect for this task and will make the job easier. Flower beds and foundation plantings look so much better with a well-defined edge. You can purchase a low fence or edging material—or simply cut the edge of the garden bed firmly and leave a good straight side, cut at an angle into the garden.

Making these neat, sharp edges around a garden is a satisfying task. It cleans up the garden so quickly and shows it off by defining where it is. I wonder how I can do that in my own life. Can I try to define where I am by defining the world around me, or is that too simplistic for today's world? How can I keep the edges smooth and straight when it seems as if I am always bending and trying to fit into the spaces around me?

Help me in this, God. Help me to see where I can smooth out parts of my life so the person I am is more obviously and evidently the person you created me to be.

"The one who sows the good seed is the Son of Man; the field is the world, and the good seed are the children of the kingdom; the weeds are the children of the evil one."

Matthew 13:37–38

Cultivate your garden regularly, at least once a week during the growing season. Otherwise the weeds will eclipse its beauty. All kinds of tools that help with the job are available. My favorite is called a swoe, a very sharp-edged tool with a long handle that gets right into the soil and breaks off weeds at the roots. If you cannot find this tool, then a hoe or a three-pronged cultivator works well, too.

The weeds in my life bind me so. They crowd me and sometimes I feel like these plants in the garden—fighting for water and nutrients with all those tenacious little weeds that would like to crowd them out of being.

Help me to cultivate the garden of my own soul, God. Teach me to recognize the parts of my personality that hold me back from giving all I can give and hold me back from receiving all I am capable of receiving. Let me know, God, what these weeds are, and then help me to cultivate my being so I am free to gather up what is ready for me to take.

The glory of youths is their strength, but the beauty of the aged is their gray hair.

Proverbs 20:29

Plastic or clay pots? I prefer the look of clay pots, but plastic pots do hold water and nutrients in the soil longer. You can try placing a plastic pot inside a clay pot, or simply use the clay and remember to water more frequently. Clay pots need a good deal of care and cleaning each season. Wash the pots with a light bleach solution once a year to make sure all chance of disease is eliminated before filling with new soil and plants.

The plastic pots work just as well as the clay, but I like my old chipped pots that have been around for many years. After so many garden seasons with me they have become like old friends. Some are covered with old moss or gray lichens that make the pots age rather beautifully. Some were given to me by gardeners who outgrew their passion and moved on to smaller quarters; they are heavy when filled with soil and I think of the people who once moved them about. These old pots are so beautiful, they wear their age well. I wish I wore my own age as well, but perhaps these pots can teach me about aging. Their simple beauty reminds me that the moss of my own life, appearing on my body these days, should be welcomed rather than shunned.

Creator, help me have the wisdom to grow old gracefully and to accept the changes that come, with as much peace as I am able.

You must follow exactly the path that the LORD your God has commanded you, so that you may live, and that it may go well with you, and that you may live long in the land that you are to possess.

Deuteronomy 5:33

Don't forget to maintain the paths in your garden. Paths often seem to emerge on their own just through wear, but you may want to actually create a path in an area that is well traveled, by placing gravel or by laying rocks or bricks. Paths can also be fashioned out of slabs cut from tree trunks or by planting a ground cover that doesn't mind being trampled. A path through a large garden can create definition and movement and add an element of design that enhances the space.

Paths pull us along. They meander, providing curves, slopes, and fresh angles. Walking a path many times becomes for me a way of prayer, a communion of spirit with God under the spell of the beauty of the garden.

God, lead me along the paths that refresh my heart and nourish my tired spirit. I may often feel lost, but when I turn to you, my guide, you show me the way of truth.

"The kingdom of heaven is like yeast that a woman took and mixed in with three measures of flour until all of it was leavened."
Matthew 13:33

I t's time to think about staking, before the plants are too big. Without stakes, flowers may be crushed by a sudden rain or wind. You can gather brush and small sticks to use as stakes, but these have to be set in place early, before the plants have leafed out. If you don't have brush, buy some bamboo stakes and plenty of green twine for the job. Sometimes well-thought-out plantings will support each other; tall lilies can be supported by an underplanting of lythrum, for example. Whatever you use for stakes, try not to bind the plants too tightly, which makes them look stiff and unnatural. You can keep a more natural look too, by covering the supports with surrounding foliage as much as possible.

Sometimes I am so stiff and unyielding, so sure I am right, that I won't listen to any other voices. I need to be able to bend, to be supple, and to not hold so firmly to my own ideas that I can't listen to anyone else. I need support to hold me up when I feel too tired to go on, and yet I don't want to be bound so closely to my idea of what is right that I don't see what God has in store for me.

Liberating One, only you know what and where your kingdom truly is; lead me there and let me be open to see it in all its guises.

The wilderness and the dry land shall be glad, the desert shall rejoice and bloom; like the crocus it shall blossom abundantly, and rejoice with joy and singing.

Isaiah 35:1–2

Is there a rocky area in your garden where little grows? Try planting a few of the smaller plants, such as sedum and the small succulents, which are known for their ability to grow among the rocks. Many botanical gardens have rock gardens where you can see what grows well in your area. Study the way the plants grow in this kind of environment and see if you can do something similar with your rocky ledge.

The rock garden and what will grow there always give me pause, when I see what survives in places that seem so inhospitable to growth. I think of all the people I see on the streets and wonder how they survive, some without means of income or a place to rest. How do they manage each day?

Give me guidance today, Source of Life, to reach out to those in need, to lend what support I can, what help I can give, be it only in prayer. Comfort them as you comfort me. As you give growth to the plants that spring from the cracks in the earth, let people find, in the dry landscape of their lives, the joy of knowing you.

Those who till their land will have plenty of food.

Proverbs 12:11

The flagstone terrace may have lots of difficult-to-control weeds growing in the cracks. If you want the look of a sterile stone area, you may have to resort to killing weeds with chemical sprays; otherwise, you can plant moss or small thyme plants amid the cracks and hope they take over. A flame gun will work on many of the annual weeds and on broadleaved perennials. Use it lightly—the idea is to heat the sap until it bursts, killing the plant.

Endless amounts of time can be spent taking weeds out of the cracks in a patio, so much time that it begins to seem foolish. I prefer letting plants grow there, rather than weeding. Those plants that grow in the cracks always seem so proud of themselves. They really struggle to grow there and do quite well.

This is a gift, God, to let things be as you want them to be. I feel so much better when I don't feel the need to control everything around me. To think I can leave this part of nature to you is wonderful indeed.

We obligate ourselves to bring the first fruits of our soil and the first fruits of all fruit of every tree, year by year, to the house of the LORD.
Nehemiah 10:35

Melons grow quickly in the hot weather. Sometimes they grow so quickly that the leaves get a bit pale, so I spray the plants with liquid fertilizer. A black plastic mulch under the melon plants can keep weeds away and provide extra heat that will help the melons ripen more quickly.

Melons are hard to grow here in the Northeast, though it is possible to get sweet ones that are worth the extra effort involved. I don't take the time to grow them every summer, but when I do, I am always glad I did. In other areas of my life, too, I need to be deliberate about taking the time to do something I will be glad I did. Maybe it will be finally stopping in to see the ninety-two-year-old woman down the road. Or it could be visiting those people I know—and maybe some I don't know—at the nursing home. It is so easy to come up with an excuse not to do tasks such as these. But when I take the time to do them I am always glad afterwards. Time is all we have, really, and though it often seems we don't have enough time in our busy lives, using it well always satisfies.

Help me, Dear God, to take my time and to share it with others.

"A man had a fig tree planted in his vineyard; and he came looking for fruit on it and found none. So he said to the gardener, 'See here! For three years I have come looking for fruit on this fig tree, and still I find none. Cut it down! Why should it be wasting the soil?' He replied, 'Sir, let it alone for one more year, until I dig around it and put manure on it. If it bears fruit next year, well and good; but if not, you can cut it down.'"

Luke 13:6–9

If you have an asparagus patch, early summer is a good time to side-dress the rows of plants with either a 10-10-10 fertilizer or a good amount of rich compost. Side-dressing, applying fertilizer or compost to the area around where the plants grow rather than directly on the plant itself, helps the plants rebuild their roots and will produce a large crop next spring.

Asparagus beds can last a long, long time, given the right kind of care each season. They send up wonderful green stalks each spring, and though the beds are a lot of work to set out, once they are established the asparagus keeps coming. Side-dressing helps and it is such a small thing to do. I compare it to what I do in my life, my own "side-dressing" of things that help me along. When I am especially ragged I realize I need to go on a short retreat to a spiritual center or retreat house where I can spend time in silence and prayer and be sustained once again for the continuous drama of everyday life. I will ask in prayer today to know when I need to plan a short break from life to be re-fed with spiritual sustenance.

Dear God, you know what I need before I do. Help me keep my whole life in order and to have the time I need to be closer to you.

If you do boast, remember that it is not you that support the root, but the root that supports you.

Romans 11:18

Buy a trellis for the garden and plant something wonderful to grow up it, a vine or a morning glory or a deep purple clematis. Put the trellis against a bare wall of the house or in a spot in the garden that could use some height and a touch of drama. I bought two trellises from a friend who makes them out of saplings and branches, and they give a certain sense of sculpture to the garden, even in the middle of the winter.

After I had placed a trellis in the garden, I wondered why I had waited so long to do so. The sudden height gives instant movement and depth to any border, especially when the flowers begin to grow up and over the frame. We all need something like a trellis in our lives, something to rest on, to grow over, and to come back to when we have reached out a bit too far and need comfort and rest.

Compassionate One, give me the support I need to go about each day knowing I have your constant comfort and love, which know no bounds. With that inner support I can do so much more. I have so much more.

I consider the days of old, and remember the years of long ago.
                                                    Psalm 77:5

A ll my pots are filled with flowers right now. I cannot decide which one I like the best. I take photographs of all of them, though. It is a good idea to take frequent pictures of your garden and the different plantings and color combinations you have tried. You can refer to them later on and remember what worked and what needed a bit of help.

☙❀

Photographs can instantly bring a garden back to mind and help in planning next year's planting scheme. Old photographs bring back other memories for me, bring people I love back to me, reminding me of a life I thought I had forgotten. After my father died, my daughters and I spent night after night looking over the photographs we found in his house. They always made us cry, and yet they gave us a sense of him in all the different stages of his life. The pictures cannot bring him back to us, but they help ease the pain, bringing back the memories of what he meant in our lives.

Dear God, I thank you for being able to recall all the times in my life that are important to me. What a gift memory is and how painful when we see a loved one lose the ability to remember. Help those, God, who suffer from memory loss. Help their families who sometimes go unremembered.

So Saul said to his servants, "Provide for me someone who can play well, and bring him to me."

                                                    1 Samuel 16:17

T ake time to play in the garden. Or roll on the grass. Find a child and play ring-around-the-rosy on the lawn or hide-and-seek behind the hedges and tall shrubs. Pick the flowers and make a crown or a beautiful necklace. Bring an armload of flowers inside to grace the dining room table. Find bare branches, place them in a vase, and notice their graceful symmetry. Enjoy what you have planted. Revel in it.

The saint is one who somehow manages to keep the serious and the playful in balance. I know that there is a light side to Christianity. I read of it in the Gospel, the "good news" that the victory has already been won. There is also a heavy side to the life of faith. I think of the many grave passages in Scripture that seem to be meant to keep me on my toes. But I need to balance the heavy and the light, to be pulled to earth and to reach up to the heavens. I need to know how to play and how to have respect for the serious. I learn this best from the older saints I know in my life. These older people seem to have the wisdom of balance; they live serenely between heaven and earth and avoid the extremes of lightness and heaviness.

Dear God, let me learn that artful balance no matter how long it takes. Let me take my faith seriously, but let me take time, too, to revel in it.

I am the vine, you are the branches. Those who abide in me and I in them bear much fruit, because apart from me you can do nothing.
John 15:5

I f you have any grapevines, they may need some tending in midsummer. Check for insect damage and get help if you notice any problems that you may not be sure how to control. Check that the vines are well supported and firmly attached to their stakes.

I have an old grapevine that doesn't produce much fruit anymore. I keep it mainly for the way it grows. It twists and curves around a trellis, arching its way over and showing forth beautiful leaves. I like it because it is old and reminds me of so many metaphors and stories. The vineyard of the Bible represents a foretaste of the glory to come; vines budding or blossoming are symbols of the land of Israel and signify happiness and peace. Jesus identified himself as the vine, offering paradise to all who would drink the pure wine of love. We are part of the vine and need the vine to live a full life. We cannot do it alone.

Dear God, you who renew my heart's gladness, lead me to the vineyards where I can learn to celebrate loving relationships and the gift of life.

Happy is the nation whose God is the LORD, the people whom he has chosen as his heritage.

Psalm 33:12

Pick vegetables and herbs when they are in their prime. Take the vegetables when they're young and tender. Don't wait until they are big and mature; enjoy them at their peak. At the height of the harvest, you will probably have to pick and prune daily.

As I pick all these gifts from the Provider, all these fruits and flowers of God's love, I wonder why it is that God has picked me.

I do feel chosen, Lord, chosen to know you and chosen to be close to you through the earth, through the garden, and through the people all around me. I know you are here for me to choose as well. How can I live so that others will know you and choose you, too? God who has picked me, help me to live as one of your chosen—and as one who teaches others that they are your chosen as well.

Fall

For everything there is a season, and a time for every matter under heaven: a time to be born, and a time to die; a time to plant, and a time to pluck up what is planted.

Ecclesiastes 3:1–2

If you like to bring your geraniums inside for the winter but find they don't do well, you may want to try taking cuttings of the plants now so you will have young, healthy plants to bring indoors. Snap off a piece about three inches long and strip each stem of all but four of the top leaves. Leave the stems exposed to the air for a day to dry the ends of the stems and keep them from rotting. Root in sand or vermiculite in pots, leave inside on a window ledge, and in about three weeks or so they can be planted in regular potting soil.

Perhaps we make cuttings so plants won't die. We who so fear death want to keep the people and things we love nearby for as long as we can. But if life is God's gift to us, then death, too, is a part of the normal human experience. We all will die. Death is natural and part of the life cycle. We mourn the life lost, but we know through our faith in the Resurrection that there is no final death; life will go on. The person we mourn still lives within us and is part of us always. We can honor the memory of loved ones in a special way by planting living memorials to them.

———————— 🌿 ————————

Dear God, thank you for this precious gift of life. Comfort us when death is near. Remind us that you offer life everlasting.

I am a rose of Sharon, a lily of the valleys.

Song of Solomon 2:1

If you have roses and live in the north, stop feeding them in the late summer. Don't prune the roses in the fall as it encourages growth that will only be killed in the winter's frost. You will want the last roses of summer to mature to hips rather than cutting them off the stem. This helps slow the rose plants down a bit in the fall and prepares them for winter.

Why do I bother with these finicky roses that don't like to grow in my garden? Some years I don't replace the ones I lose each spring. But there are two old climbers that have been here for at least thirty years. They nearly failed a few years ago, but now, with some care and prodding, they are doing well again, offering their small, profuse clusters of pink blooms each summer. They won't win any prizes, but I like them and the way they stick it out when their fairer cousins cannot survive.

Help me too, God, prepare for the winter season of my life. I may be active now but who knows what may lie ahead? Let me remember what this feels like, to be in my prime, to be doing all I want to do and to be so happy with the world around me. Guide me in what ways are best to be ready for times less bountiful, and remind me always of your presence.

So Jesus came out, wearing the crown of thorns and the purple robe. Pilate said to them, "Here is the man!"

John 19:5

Perhaps you have some thorny berry bushes in your yard as I do. Be sure to trim these regularly or they will take over the garden. I use long-handled loppers for this job, but for some of the finer work I need to get in close with my pocket clippers. Be sure to wear heavy gloves for the clipping. The plants look so much better when the job is done that I am always glad I did it, no matter how difficult it seemed at first.

The thorns I encounter, of course, are not all in my garden. Why are some people such thorns to us? How do they manage to prick us so in the most aggravating way possible? And why am I sometimes a thorn to others?

Dear Friend and Helping God, the One whom I constantly call on, let me notice the thorns I rub against today. Help me to recognize why they bother me and to see what is in me that causes that grievance. Help me to pray when I come upon them and, when necessary, help me to clip them out of my life. Give me guidance to see this, no matter how painful it may be.

Protect me, O God, for in you I take refuge.

Psalm 16:1

A good way to beat the weeds is to mulch the plants in the garden. A thick mulch stops weeds from germinating by preventing sunlight from reaching the weeds. Mulch also keeps moisture in the soil so plants won't dry out as fast. Mulch two to three weeks after planting in order to allow the soil to warm first and the plants to sprout. There are many materials to use as mulch: in the vegetable garden, try a cover of straw or salt hay; in flower beds try small chips of wood or buckwheat hulls.

❧

Spreading the mulch carefully around the plants and between the rows gives me a measure of contentment that is difficult to name. I think of mulch as a thick blanket, covering the earth and protecting the plants from drought and lack of cultivation. Maybe that's one reason I enjoy this chore. It is a simple task and yet it accomplishes so much. As I tuck the plants in, it reminds me of tucking my daughters into bed at night, making sure they are safe, kissing their foreheads and saying prayers. No matter how old I get, I want that feeling of safety too, that feeling of being tucked into bed, where no one can harm me.

———————— 🍃 ————————

Dear God, hold me and cover me today with your warmth and love. Let me know that I am never alone. Keep me close, keep me close.

Do not neglect to do good and to share what you have, for such sacrifices are pleasing to God.

Hebrews 13:16

S hare some of the bounty of the garden today. Pack a basket with the produce you cannot use and give it to someone who needs it or someone who doesn't have a garden. You can do this in remembrance of St. Claire, a saint known for her devotion to "holy poverty," a saint who would be happy to see us give what we have too much of, as she lived her life in complete austerity. St. Claire was happy living in devotion to the Lord and needed little else.

Many of us in this culture have so much of everything. We are consumed with it and by it. Sometimes during my prayer time I find myself thinking of recent purchases or of things I might buy, rather than of God. What is this disease? For it is surely a disease in ourselves and our society that by buying and consuming we feel better. And then, of course, we feel better only for the moment. Our relationship with God is all that can really fill our hearts and our beings with the peace we are after.

———————— 🌿 ————————

Fill us, God, fill us until we can show and share your love with others. Maybe then we will be able to give away all that we do not really need.

For thus says the Lord to the people of Judah and to the inhabitants of Jerusalem: Break up your fallow ground, and do not sow among thorns.
Jeremiah 4:3

Be sure to keep putting the waste of the garden into the compost pile. If you don't have one, start one now. Store kitchen waste in a bucket in the kitchen that you can carry out to the pile every other day. If you live in an area where a large pile may be too unsightly for the neighbors, consider making a compost pile in a large garbage can with holes cut into the bottom or in a wooden box that can be aerated at the top and bottom.

❧

There is so much waste in our lives that we can barely see around it, yet sometimes what seems like trash in our lives may not be. It may really be something that can help us, the way rich compost helps the garden. The challenge is in learning to recognize the difference, to know what we really need in our lives and what is of little use.

Dear God, help me eliminate addictions and habits that are not productive, that do not yield any fruit in my life. Let me instead nurture those gifts I have that can be of some benefit to others around me: my ability to listen, my ability to be a quiet presence in the midst of chaos. Let the things that bring me peace and comfort thrive under your care.

"When it is evening you say, 'It will be fair weather, for the sky is red.' And in the morning, 'It will be stormy today, for the sky is red and threatening.' You know how to interpret the appearance of the sky, but you cannot interpret the signs of the times."

Matthew 16:2–3

Early fall is the season of downpours, when the rain comes along fast, soaking into the earth. When it is raining can be a good time to be in the garden (unless, of course, it's in the middle of an electrical storm). Weeds come up easily in the rain, and plants like to be planted when there is gentle rainfall. But often the storms are so strong and the rains so heavy that many plants need to be supported against them. It is important to stake those plants with sturdy poles or thick saplings before the rains come.

I need support too. Not all the storms in my life are very serious but some do seem terrifying.

Help me, God my Protector, to weather the storms in my life and to be able to find refuge where I can be united with all others and with you. Let me be held up even when the winds are strong.

The God who has girded me with strength has opened wide my path.
                                                        2 Samuel 22:33

This is a good time to check your garden paths. Do the paths work? Do they go where you want them to go? Do you need a path somewhere? Getting rid of a path is simple—just cover it with soil and create a new flower bed. If you see a path in the lawn that you didn't plan on, but the ground is obviously well worn, it may suggest the need for a real path, one of gravel or stone.

Some would say that a garden becomes a garden once there is a path through it. I find a path gives a perspective for discovering plants from different angles, and pulls me along the landscape of the garden. When I walk it again and again, the path becomes part of me. Walking along a path slowly becomes a form of meditation. Even a short path in a small garden is worthwhile. I stand there gazing at the garden, forgetting all my concerns.

Dear Guide and Deliverer, show me the paths in my own life that can lead me to places of refreshment and growth. Steer and guide me along the way so I am never alone. Help me travel those routes that I may hesitate to take but that I know may lead to new understandings. Show me the path to you, God, and help me today to tread it lightly.

May those who sow in tears reap with shouts of joy. Those who go out weeping, bearing the seed for sowing, shall come home with shouts of joy, carrying their sheaves.

Psalm 126:5–6

During the late summer and early fall you will need to harvest your vegetable garden regularly. Check your beans every day and pick them before the beans begin to bulge, or they will turn tough and stringy. Picking the ripe beans encourages the plants to continue flowering so you can have more and more beans to eat. Picking vegetables at just the right time is the key to the garden harvest. You can buy beans at the store, but you cannot buy small, tender, wonderful beans picked at the point of perfection. That's the reason behind all this work!

Life is so full and so rich. Sometimes I need to take stock of my own life and keep harvesting the spiritual gifts that seem to keep coming. I often find that when the harvest is rich in my own spiritual life I feel so full that I need to spend time thinking and praying and dwelling on why this is so.

Help me to listen, Lord. Let me spend as much time as possible reflecting on the many gifts you constantly offer me. Let me continually harvest the bounty that comes again and again from you in my own prayers.

A garden fountain, a well of living water, and flowing streams from Lebanon.

Song of Solomon 4:15

Garden ponds need to be cleaned at least once a year. If it is a small pond, used for decorative purposes, clean out any dead vegetation lying on the surface of the water at the end of summer. Then cover the surface with a fine plastic netting. This allows light to come through but will collect the dead leaves of fall and prevent them from polluting the water. The netting can be taken up and cleaned and replaced as needed.

✿

Ponds can be pools of reflection for our lives, places to sit near and meditate—or they can become clogged with leaves and turn into smelly eyesores! They take work, like everything else in the garden, but usually the work is worth the effort.

Dear God, help me to keep my prayer life clear and let me reflect on my relationship with you in my daily life. Let me appear to others as I want to appear to you. When I feel clouded, help me to be clear.

"It is like a mustard seed, which, when sown upon the ground, is the smallest of all the seeds on earth; yet when it is sown it grows up and becomes the greatest of all shrubs, and puts forth large branches, so that the birds of the air can make nests in its shade."

Mark 4:31–32

T hink about planting a shrub in the early fall, giving the plant enough time to settle in before winter arrives. If it turns windy, protect the plant with burlap or screening so it survives through the first season. A wonderful variety of shrubs is available; some offer fruit for birds, others are quite fragrant, and others have colored bark that delights all winter long. Do some exploring!

🌿

Shrubs are part of the bones of the garden, the parts of the garden that don't die back in the winter but give structure even when snow arrives. When you are choosing your shrubs, therefore, consider what they will look like in years to come. Look for plants with graceful shapes or lines that will add to the design you want to create.

These shrubs remind me, God, of the parts of my life that I take for granted—my home, my health, and the family I love. I wake up each morning giving thanks for them, but I know they aren't secure. They could change. We lose parts of our lives all the time. What then is the real bone, the real structure in my own life? I think it is what you have given me, God, the knowledge of you and your love. Be with me today, and let me rest secure in your love, knowing that I am safe, whatever may happen in the world around me.

"I will put my spirit within you, and you shall live, and I will place you on your own soil; then you shall know that I, the LORD, have spoken and will act," says the LORD.

Ezekiel 37:14

Consider sowing a source of nitrogen into your vegetable garden. Sowing clover seed in rows or broadcasting it over an empty bed and then raking it in lightly provides your garden with a good winter cover. In addition to preventing erosion, the clover helps the nitrogen in the soil when it is turned under.

Sowing nitrogen sounds fairly impressive to me. I wonder what growers did before they knew about such things as sowing nitrogen in the soil. Did they just have such an affinity with the earth that they knew what worked and what didn't? Wouldn't it be something to know the soil so well that you could feel it and look at it and know just what the plants would want and what the soil lacked?

Knowing what the garden needs comes from our connection to the earth. What a gift it is for us to be able to be close to nature, for when our eyes are open to see the many gifts all around us, it is easy to rejoice and feel closer to the Creator.

———————— 🍃 ————————

Dear God, give me the grace today to feel, as I work in the soil and crumble it beneath my fingers, that I am beginning to know it. Let me take the time, Lord, to truly be in the garden, feeling it around me, letting it tell me its story. If I am still enough, I can find you here, near my heart, near this soil.

And after he had dismissed the crowds, he went up the mountain by him-self to pray. When evening came, he was there alone.

Matthew 14:23

Before the first frost, it is a good idea to move your houseplants back indoors. If they have been in a sunny spot, move them into the shade for a few days before you take them inside to accustom them gradually to lower light levels. Make the move indoors on a day when the outdoor temperatures are close to the indoor temperatures of your house. Sometimes an interim move to a garage or sun porch is a good idea. Inspect each plant for bugs and clean the plant well before you take it inside.

The change of seasons reminds me that life is a series of constant changes. Like my plants, however, I often need some transitional time to help me get from what is old to what is new. As the fall approaches, I like to take a day of silence to think about what I want for the days to come and how I want to spend my spare time. Another year has begun.

Children are off to school; activities are starting again. What do I want this fall? What can I do in my prayer life to help me along the way? How can I deepen my time with God? A day of silence helps me focus on these questions and make the transition more smoothly.

Dear God, be with me as the days shorten and become cooler. Guide me into the quiet of the upcoming season by letting me listen now to the silence around me. Let me draw on that silence to find peace within.

On either side of the river is the tree of life with its twelve kinds of fruit, producing its fruit each month; and the leaves of the tree are for the healing of the nations.

Revelation 22:2

Raking becomes almost a daily chore once the leaves start falling. If you don't remove the leaves from the lawn, they will compact and kill the grass. (Oak leaves, however, are an exception to the rule and can be raked into the garden as a good cover for the winter ahead.) Pile all leaves, shredded, into the compost, or make separate piles of leaf mold, shredded leaves that are left to sit over the winter and used in the spring as broken-down compost to boost the soil. Or, if you need extra insulation around the house, fill large bags with leaves and bank the foundation for an extra layer of warmth.

It takes time for these leaves to break down so that they can add nutrients to the soil and perhaps even feed the trees from which they fell. It is all a cycle; the leaves fall and ultimately feed the new ones that come in the spring. As I rake fallen leaves and prepare the garden for winter sleep, I focus on the passage of life and signs of death and pray that I'll live my days fully.

———————— 🌿 ————————

Dear God of Life and Death, let me give priority to the things most important and make better use of my hours. When the morning breaks, let me depend even more on your love as I observe the wondrous, perfect cycle you have created.

As he came out of the temple, one of his disciples said to him, "Look, Teacher, what large stones and what large buildings!" Then Jesus asked him, "Do you see these great buildings? Not one stone will be left here upon another; all will be thrown down."

Mark 13:1–2

A s the busyness in the garden lessens somewhat, look at the garden with a critical eye and think about spots that need a little something. Maybe a large rock would fill the space nicely. Stones can be focal points in a garden and can complete a picture, often complementing plant material that is already there.

Smaller stones can be precious mementos and even tokens to help with prayer. Holding a stone as you pray may help you focus and concentrate. Let your fingers wander over the surface of the stone as your mind goes over and over the words or the nonwords of your prayer. Stones can be objects to focus on, to meditate on as well. Think about where the stones have been and why you happened to pick up the one you did. How did it get into your hands? How did God give it to you? What memories does the stone evoke?

———————— 🌿 ————————

Dear God, let me think of you as I hold this small smooth stone that has been here for so many more years than I have. Each time I touch it, let it remind me of you.

Ground that drinks up the rain falling on it repeatedly, and that produces a good crop useful to those for whom it is cultivated, receives a blessing from God.

Hebrews 6:7

Soil is so important to the overall health of a garden. Toward the end of the growing season add some organic matter, such as manure or compost, to enrich the soil for next year's planting. Test and correct the soil's pH level at this time of year, too. Vegetables like a pH level of about 6.8. Usually you have to add ground limestone to achieve this number. Add it at the rate of five pounds per hundred square feet.

Often I have to test myself to see how I am really feeling. What is my pH level? Am I feeling empty, or do I have a sense of the Holy within? When I feel rather limp, I may need some replenishing with a retreat, a time to be alone with the Holy in prayer and meditation. Or, perhaps now is a good time to find a spiritual director to help me on my journey.

Someone well versed in listening to the landscape of my prayer and seeing where it is going could help tremendously in seeing how God is acting in my life.

Dear God, I pray today for guidance in seeking what I need to meet the Holy.

Likewise the Spirit helps us in our weakness; for we do not know how to pray as we ought, but that very Spirit intercedes with sighs too deep for words.

Romans 8:26

Do you have a good work surface in the house or garage for your gardening needs? A good work surface is important for sowing seeds, repotting plants, and all sorts of other jobs that can be done indoors. You want a table that can stand lots of abuse, so one made out of a sheet of plywood or one you find at a garage sale might work well. Keep pots nearby and hang tools on the wall. Make sure you have some potting soil on hand. I store mine in a large, covered, heavy-plastic container.

❧

I know I need the basics before I begin gardening and then it's just time and effort to get the results that I want. Praying is like that, too. I have the basics within; the desire for more is there. That emptiness I have that I cannot fill by buying things or acquiring more and more is there, and prayer always fills it. God's Spirit is just waiting to be called upon, waiting to be asked to be part of my life. I can start each day by taking my desires to God. The one I take today is my desire to have my self made whole, and I ask for God's help with that.

———————— 🌿 ————————

Dear God, you know me so much better than I know myself. Help me use what I have, these rude beginnings and basic tools, to better find you in my life. Help me in my prayer and in my longing to take the time to hear you and to listen to what your word is telling me.

Winter

And this is my prayer, that your love may overflow more and more with knowledge and full insight to help you to determine what is best, so that in the day of Christ you may be pure and blameless.

Philippians 1:9–10

Planning a vegetable garden can be fun, especially during the times of year when you cannot get outdoors. Write down all the vegetables you would like to have growing in the garden and, using your catalogs and a garden reference, determine each plant's growing needs and space requirements. Make your vegetable garden a real kitchen garden by adding flowers and herbs in those small spaces.

✳

My garden plans sometimes get translated directly into the garden, but other times, once I start planting, the plan is all but forgotten. Plans that work are those that don't ask too much of our resources of time or energy. At this time of year we seem to think we can do a great deal more than we may really be able to do.

I ask for help today with this, God, help in discerning what I can do in my life and what is too difficult for me. So much seems possible when I have you in my life that I can get carried away. Lead me, Lord, to what it is that you want me to do. Help me to know which path I need to choose. Let me be open in prayer to hear your voice.

"As long as the earth endures, seedtime and harvest, cold and heat, summer and winter, day and night, shall not cease."

Genesis 8:22

S ometimes in the winter we have a thaw that is okay for plants as long as they are well protected. Alternate freezing and thawing of the earth can cause plants to heave out of the ground. If you have perennials and are expecting a thaw and the ground is not covered with a thick blanket of snow, be sure the plants are protected with a mulch of evergreen boughs or salt hay.

✳

The warmer days in the winter are good for getting out and walking, observing the world in its stillness and noticing the different types of bark and the shapes of the trees and shrubs. The blankets of protection given to my plants are also ones that I crave—and not only at this time of year.

In prayer today, God, I ask you for that added layer of comfort I so desire. Sometimes I don't even know I need it and then in prayer the word comfort seems to come to me, enfolding me with the simple knowledge of the truth. I give this desire to you, God, and I ask you to put your arms around me; cover me and keep me warm.

The light shines in the darkness, and the darkness did not overcome it.
John 1:5

Plant—or plan—a moon garden, a garden of white flowered plants and plants with silvery foliage that glisten in the moonlight. Depending on where you live, you can choose from a wide variety of plants. A friend of mine has planted her moon garden with three birch trees right outside her window. At night she likes to ponder this garden, which seems lit from within. The trees remind her of the Trinity, and the white cosmos, snapdragons, and silvery artemesia seem to come alive when all else bows out for the day.

✴

---✶---

God, give me the magic that I see in this garden that seems to light up at night. Let me be lit from within and let the glow from your love shine forth. Be my light, dear God, when darkness falls and again when the day is new.

"Blessed are those who mourn, for they will be comforted."
Matthew 5:4

When I was lucky enough to have a small greenhouse attached to my house, I grew lettuce year round. If you have such a spot, or even a cold frame, you can grow greens in rich soil quite easily. Simply sow at intervals throughout the fall, and you can harvest well into the winter. It is important to use deep planters of rich soil. Add nutrients if you plant more than one crop during this season. Harvest by clipping away the outer leaves of the lettuce plants, and the plants will last longer.

✳

I long for the sun and the warmth on these cold, bleak days when I am feeling especially alone. Sometimes in prayer I am so silent that I can only hope that somehow God still hears my plea for protection.

Dear Comforter, let the Spirit come and bring my prayers to you, prayers I am not even fully aware of. Protect me as this greenhouse shelters the plants from the harsh winter weather. Stay with me now and surround me with the warmth that only you can give.

Upon you I have leaned from my birth.... My praise is continually of you.
Psalm 71:6

You can create some interesting landscapes by using one plant to support another. What about using that crabapple tree as a support for a variegated euonymus plant? Euonymus likes to climb and before long will wrap itself around the tree, giving a wonderful look to the garden. Try this with other vines, such as clematis or the annual morning glory. Let the plants entwine around larger plants that are already mainstays in the landscape.

✳

The tree offers support to the vine, which clings by its tendrils to the higher branches. I compare it to my rule of life, something that supports me each day. A rule of life is like a contract you make with yourself, with God, and sometimes with other people. It is a guide that you can keep or easily go back to if you should stray. It helps give my spiritual life a sense of purpose. Part of my rule is starting each day with prayer. This daily prayer is a support and balance without which I stumble.

Dear God, help me to live my faith as you would want me to and to live my life through you and in you from this day forward. Grant me the persistence I need to keep my contract so that I am supported in all the ways I need.

I am grateful to God—whom I worship with a clear conscience, as my ances-tors did—when I remember you constantly in my prayers night and day.
                                                                    2 Timothy 1:3

An important part of gardening is taking care of the tools that make the job all the easier. Fall is a good time to clean your tools before you put them away for the winter. Oil and rub handles and metal tines. Sharpen whatever needs sharpening. Remove all surface dirt. Put tools away carefully. Hang them on the wall or keep them in covered contain-ers where they will be safe and dry until next season.

✳

Thank heaven for these tools! I give a special prayer of thanks for each shovel and hoe as I clean each one and remember where it came from. Spiritual tools are also important to me: the ability to pray, the gift of the Holy Spirit, the joy of finding God in life around me, the chance to talk to a spiritual director about how God is acting in my life—the list goes on and on!

———— ✳ ————

These tools give me the ability to reach out to you, Lord, for I know you yearn for me as you yearn for each one of us. Your yearning fills me with love and sureness of heart. Let me keep these tools sharp by constant use, Dear One, and help me to use them with greater discernment.

But if we hope for what we do not see, we wait for it with patience.
Romans 8:25

Gardens take time to grow and to mature to what they are meant to be. We often make the mistake of planting young plants much too close together, only to have to move them in a year or two when they have grown to a fuller size. When you plan a border, you need to consider the eventual size of the plants even though it can be difficult to imagine them at maturity. Read about the plants you are thinking of using, and learn what size they will become. At planting time, give them the space they will need, and then wait patiently for the garden to grow.

✴

A garden cannot be pushed or hurried along. Neither can my own spiritual growth be rushed, much as I would like that to be so. There will be seasons of plenty, seasons of drought, seasons of blossom, seasons of winter snows and seeming blankness.

Lord, take away my notion of control and teach me to be patient, mindful that everything comes in its own due season and time. Help me to bear with the difficult and more barren seasons and patiently await the flowering of new life that will come again.

The word is very near to you; it is in your mouth and in your heart for you to observe.

Deuteronomy 30:14

Plant something new in the garden, or buy a houseplant you have never tried before and see how it grows. Tending for a new plant can teach us about another aspect of gardening we may not have considered before. It is never too late to learn something new. Plants can teach us a great deal.

✳

I am always learning, always learning about how much I don't know! I feel sometimes as if I have so far to go in prayer, in learning to be still, in living each day for the moment, and in being aware of all the signs of the Spirit in my daily life.

———————— ✳ ————————

Let me learn from these plants, God, something I need to know. Lead me into new dimensions of my life by helping me to settle into what is already before me and to learn and rethink all I think I already know.